The Waterfront House

The Waterfront House

LIVING WITH STYLE ON THE COAST

PHOEBE HOWARD

WRITTEN WITH ANDREW SESSA

ABRAMS, NEW YORK

FOR MY GRANDCHILDREN:
JACK, HENRY, ROSIE, VIOLET,
BRODY, JOE, AND LIAM

Contents

Introduction

i didn't grow up in a house on the water, but I did grow up at the beach. Nearly every day of my childhood, my four brothers and I would race from our home three doors away from the ocean in North Florida and spend hours upon hours in the sand, the surf, the sun. We were the ultimate water babies, and we had the sunburned noses to prove it.

The houses I saw on the beach—with their patios and porches; their wooden walls indoors and out, often painted a cool white; and their palettes pulled from their oceanfront settings—all very much influenced how I design today. In every home I decorate, I look for ways to seamlessly connect interior and outdoor spaces to encourage alfresco living and entertaining. And there's nothing I love more than a soothing color scheme of pale blues and light greens set off by the whites, ivories, and other neutrals you see in the shades of seashells, dried seagrass, driftwood, and the sand that surrounds them. When I select prints and materials, I look for those that echo the subtle shimmer of sun on water, the movement of waves across the sea, and the patterns and textures those waves leave in their wake.

Every time I look at the water, I find new inspiration. And that was true even before I had a waterfront house of my own. Though I dreamed of it since my earliest days, decades would pass before I actually moved into one, first on the Saint Johns River in Jacksonville and then in Jacksonville Beach, where my husband, Jim, and I recently finished a house.

And I've got to tell you, I've never felt more at peace. There's just something about waking up on the water—the sound of it moving and the way the light reflects off it through the windows—that soothes my soul. I never grow tired of it. And I'm not alone. According to a wealth of scientific research, a nice view of water is good for you. The sense of peace and calm it creates offers loads of benefits for your mental and emotional wellbeing.

Living on the water also keeps me from being lazy, both creatively and physically. The constantly changing vistas are like a painting that's different every day, inspiring me anew, and an invigorating walk on the beach is always waiting for me just over the dunes. How could I stay inside?

Long before living in my own waterfront house, I'd decorated scores of them, and I've learned a thing or two about what makes them work. Their owners and I want them to be pretty, of course—and they certainly are—but they've got to be practical, too. In fact, when you're designing on the water, be it a lake or a river, and especially on the ocean, practicality has got to be considered as much as prettiness.

But don't worry if that doesn't sound like much fun. I'm here with the good news that the logistical challenges and concerns of waterfront living all give way to creative decorating opportunities and beautiful design solutions. And in this book, I'm going to share with you all I've learned about combining the practical with the pretty when designing on the water—and in ways that hide the former while accentuating the latter.

Because here's the thing we can't ignore: Houses on the water must withstand the elements more than those in any other setting. They just do. There are the challenges of wind and water, to be sure, but also those of sudden spills and sandy feet and never enough storage space.

And that's because the best waterfront houses are resort-like retreats—designed for a crowd and for a good time. These homes exist to spark joy. And *that's* really the most important thing to keep your eye on. Party houses in the most sophisticated sense, these homes are meant not just to be lived in. They get to be *enjoyed* by the generations of families who call them home—plus the friends, neighbors, and assorted other guests who are always stopping by.

That's long been the case but has been amplified recently: people have raced to buy houses on the water, seeking the salve of their soothing settings. And they're building homes big enough to gather with all the folks they care about.

When Jim and I were designing and building our own house on the beach, we increased its size and its amenities again and again. And now that it's done, with our four kids, their spouses, and our seven—and counting!—grandkids, we're empty nesters no more. And I couldn't be happier.

Everyone wants to be over at our place. I'd say it's about my company and my cooking—and it used to be—but now it's all about the pool and that sand and sun and surf. They check in to Hotel Howard at 9:00 a.m., and they don't leave till sundown or after, no matter how many times Jim asks (only half kiddingly) when they're leaving.

Though I get a bit embarrassed about how many towels we go through, I don't even care when my kids and grandkids mess everything up—I've designed it all to be easy to clean, hard to damage, and relatively inexpensive to replace if, and when, replacement is required. That keeps the carefree focus on family, fun, and togetherness.

And that, of course, is right where our focus should be, wherever you live—but nowhere more so than when you live on the water.

Hobe Sound

a blissful serenity characterizes every corner of this seasonal house. It owes much of that to where it sits, on a small bluff overlooking the Intracoastal Waterway's gently flowing Indian River on Florida's eastern shores, just outside of Jupiter. In contrast to the relative hustle and bustle and Atlantic Ocean surf of Jupiter proper, this enclave exudes tranquility. And the house does, too. That's because architect Christian Thomas, of the firm Thomas | Melhorn, and I took the peaceful location—along with the Michigan-based husband-and-wife homeowners' request for a relaxed warm-weather refuge—as our guides.

As much as the home is filled with a sense of calm, it's also filled with wonderful memories. The property, whose views extend over the water to a pristine nature pre-serve, had long belonged to the husband's parents. He cherished the recollections he had of it: spending time with his family there, staying in the guesthouse both when he and his wife were a young couple and later with their small children. Because of this emotional attachment, he wanted to preserve something of what he remembered, even though the original house required more updating than even a gut renovation could provide and had to be replaced.

The new house—inspired by Barbadian Georgian architecture and featuring high-ceilinged, light-filled spaces and large windows and glass doors that blur the line between indoors and out—doesn't match the humbler aesthetic of the old. But the

My favorite feature of this home's entry? The way the arched front door is mirrored by the curved opening to the living room. PREVIOUS PAGES: Set just outside of Jupiter, Florida, the property features lush gardens leading to the Intracoastal Waterway.

The rich hues of the moody Wellon
Bridgers artwork over the mantel
help to ground the living room's airy,
light-blue and pale-sand hues.

design still very much captures the warm feelings and lovely memories of family quality time. As the husband likes to say to visitors now, "We wanted the new house to be exactly the same, only entirely different!"

Built upon the foundations of the former residence, the new one encourages informal gatherings in the large living room, big dinners on the loggia, and evenings spent outdoors together by the pool, enjoying the gentle breeze while the sun slips slowly below the horizon and boats pass by.

When it came to designing the interiors, I wanted to combine then and now by mixing nostalgia for the past with excitement about the present and hope for the future. That meant filling the spaces with a carefully curated assortment of furnishing, both antique and new, using shapes, colors, and materials that echoed the serene setting. I used pale blues pulled from the surrounding waters to define the scene throughout, along with light neutral hues, natural materials, and soft textures.

In almost every room, the water views command the most attention. Everything, and I mean everything, here plays to those vistas, which make a big statement as soon

OPPOSITE AND FOLLOWING PAGES: The wood paneling of the entryway climbs
to the ceiling in the living room, where I mixed stripes with medallion
and lattice prints. The flat-weave rug has proven easy to keep clean.

ABOVE: The kitchen's bar area was painted the same tone as the wood paneling, which helps it look like part of the adjoining hall. OPPOSITE: We kept every surface in the kitchen matte and marvelous, from the lime-washed walls to the burnished-pewter range hood and the unlacquered brass hardware.

The breakfast area's banquette is so deep and comfortable, it's basically a sofa. (I set two tables at it to make it easier to get in and out of.) I love the playful atmosphere created by the big Isamu Noguchi paper lantern and the curving rush backs of the chairs.

as you come in the front door. You can look through the large living room to see right out to the water beyond three sets of French doors. We lovingly selected all of the furniture here—the woven-rope chairs upholstered in a blue-and-white medallion block print, the ivory-hued sofa, the spindle-framed chair—but your eyes will almost cast right over all of it to the water. And that's just what they're supposed to do.

Because the guesthouse has fewer direct water vistas, we could play a bit more there with brighter colors, slightly quirky accessories, and a bit of a 1960s and '70s vibe. We didn't have to worry about those elements distracting from the waterfront setting.

Both the vintage style and brighter color scheme of the guesthouse come from a painting the owners asked me to use as inspiration. It belonged to the husband's parents, and they remembered it fondly. I borrowed the piece's retro look and vibrant palette for the lime, tangerine, and cerulean hues here. The more playful atmosphere they help create makes this new guesthouse an especially fun getaway for visitors. I particularly love the ceramic parrots from the owners' collection, which we placed on the covered porch's dining table.

The couple hoped the whole property would feel calm, cozy, and livable—the furthest thing from dressy and precious. And that's exactly what we gave them. The new house maintains the warm Old Florida feel of the original home while incorporating modern comfort, convenience, and style in the reimagined design.

OPPOSITE AND PREVIOUS PAGES: The house is on the calm Intracoastal, so we could use relatively delicate outdoor furniture, like the coffee table made from a tiled antique panel. Keith Williams of the celebrated landscape design firm Nievera Williams created the lush tropical gardens.

The slim proportions of this plaster four-poster bed—from the collection my husband, Jim, and I designed for Sherrill Furniture—accomplish the neat trick of appearing monumental but barely there at the same time. It elegantly enhances the ample space of the primary bedroom.

Designing a
PRIMARY BATHROOM

Mix masculine and feminine. Because the bathroom in a home's primary suite often serves both men and women, it needs to be balanced and relatively neutral. Here, I combined the gentle curves of the tub and the architecture with the angles of the ottoman and the floor's grid.

Let tile be your rug. I love to design a tile floor for a bathroom that's as visually interesting as a rug—which is certainly the case here, where a combination of marble tiles creates a plaid pattern.

Match materials. You don't see wood-paneled walls in a bathroom all that often. But because they're used in so many places throughout this house, they were just the thing to use here—albeit sparingly, in the arch above the bath—to create a sense of continuity from room to room.

Reveal and conceal. Cafe curtains are my go-tos in a bathroom, especially when you live on the water. They protect your privacy while also letting in at least some of the lovely local light and coastal views.

Keep them separated. I love my husband, but I don't love sharing a sink or even counter space with him, which is why I always divide the two sinks in a primary bath onto two totally different vanities, often across the room from each other. (Though you can't see them, that's the way they are here.)

Light it up. Light is essential in a bathroom, and you need as much as possible. If you don't have the lovely natural light of this one (and even this one doesn't at night), you'll want a combination of ceiling pendants, recessed fixtures, and sconces.

OPPOSITE: I love to put an ottoman in a primary bathroom. It's a great spot to take shoes on and off, apply lotion, or place extra towels. This one opens to reveal storage inside, making it even more useful. PAGE 32: A single shade of blue used in a variety of ways soothes the eye in this guest room. PAGE 33: This porch's stellar views called for simple furnishings.

OPPOSITE AND FOLLOWING PAGES: Since the guesthouse sits right up against the pool, it can also function as something of a pool cabana when there aren't guests in residence. The architects designed its covered porch with this in mind, thinking about it as a spot to get out of the sun during lunch or while reading or napping.

Designing for
POOLSIDE LOUNGING

MAKE IT PRETTY

On a roll. There's not much of a way to make a statement with your chaises, especially if they don't have cushions. And that's just fine. Let them sit quietly. It's always nice, though, to get a beautiful pool towel and roll it into a bolster pillow on each chaise before guests arrive. It adds a thoughtful touch that makes things feel special.

Looking up. Umbrellas, however? They can make a statement. There are so many options these days: hexagons, octagons, square, round. Try doing something a little fun with a contrasting color on the inside, a scalloped or shaped valance, or some trim—even fringe.

Small wonders. I love to use glazed ceramic garden stools as tables next to chaises. They come in so many colors, patterns, and curving shapes that contrast with the straight lines of most chaises. And they're flat on top, so perfect for holding things.

MAKE IT PRACTICAL

No cushions, no problem. The number one issue with outdoor furniture is cushions—how to store them, how to dry them, how to keep them clean. That's why I prefer sling mesh for chaise lounges. It's comfortable, with some give; it dries quickly, with most water running through it; and it can be hosed right off when it gets dirty.

Have wheels, will travel. It's always a good idea to invest in chaise lounges with wheels. Their shape and size cause even the most lightweight ones to be a bit awkward for one person to balance and carry. Rolling them from one spot to another, in and out of the sun, makes things much easier.

Lighten up. In a hot, sunny climate, you'll find that dark colors, especially on chaises, get very, very hot to the touch. So, I always use hues in the lighter range—white, ivory, ecru. These tones also show much less pollen in the springtime. You'd see every speck of it on a darker color.

When picking seating to go by a swimming pool, I like to go for pieces made of mesh stretched between a metal frame, rather than those with full cushions. Water from wet bathing suits just drains right through and dries very quickly.

Duck's Nest

O riginally built in 1891 by Henry Maddock, an English importer of Chinese porcelain, Duck's Nest now stands as the second-oldest residential structure in the town of Palm Beach, Florida. But that's only the beginning of what makes this adorable little place so special.

Named for the birds that roost nearby, the house enjoys a sensational coastal position. Its west-facing views out over the Intracoastal Waterway offer up some of the best sunsets around. And its cottage-style Victorian architecture—whose evocative details include scalloped shingles, stained-glass windows, and multiple gables set off by wave-shaped moldings—provide charm to spare. When Duck's Nest came to its new twenty-first-century owners, however, it was down on its luck, held up by little more than a tree stump. Local cats had called it home for years.

It takes special people to take on a project like this, and that's just who the new owners are. Longtime lovers of Palm Beach and its history, they lived in a house just behind Duck's Nest. (I designed that one for them, too, several years prior.) They were ready to not only bring this landmark back from the brink but to do so while living up to the requirements of the town and the local historical society.

The owners painstakingly researched the house's past, using a bevy of vintage photographs they had access to. And together with architects Roger Janssen and Meghan Ford Taylor, who oversaw construction, we developed a design that remained true to the home's original aesthetic flavor. We then took the building down to the studs before putting it all back together, replacing every surface in the process: floors, walls, ceilings, you name it.

OPPOSITE AND PREVIOUS PAGES: The second oldest residence still standing in Palm Beach, the 130-year-old house known as Duck's Nest cried out for a restoration and decoration that preserved its Old Florida charm and inviting sense of whimsy.

DUCK'S

OLDEST STANDING HOU
BUILT IN 1891 BY HENRY MA
PARTS OF THE HOUSE WERE A
AND BROUGHT BY BARG
AS THIS WAS THE ONLY MEAN

MARKER PLACED BY THE T

You can't imagine the conversations we had about every decision, even beadboard: What width should it be? What direction should it run? What exactly is the finish? All our work was rewarded when the redone house received Palm Beach's prestigious Robert I. Ballinger Award for historic preservation of a landmark.

As much as its history, the home's placement on the Intracoastal Waterway guided our work. From the minute you enter the house, water is a part of it, seen through the large living room, where huge windows draw you out to a dock and the owners' beautiful blue boat. The original design, as well as its 1940 update and expansion by famed midcentury Palm Beach architect John Volk, had clearly been influenced by this

OPPOSITE, ABOVE, AND PREVIOUS PAGES: From the scalloped shingles on its facade and the thin, turned pillars of its broad front porch all the way up to the wave motifs of its fascia boards and the finials atop its petite gables, the playful sensibility of the house's architecture inspired the look and feel of its new interiors.

Designing with
VINTAGE FINDS

MAKE IT PRETTY

Mix more than match. You'll want to integrate decades-old treasures with more contemporary furniture to maintain a sense of balance while also letting vintage finds stand out. Wicker, rattan, bamboo, and painted pieces all look great near the water. The trick is to incorporate a balanced blend of all four.

A coat of paint and new fabric go a long way. Coastal antiques often have a sense of whimsy, adding levity to your design, especially if you update them with fresh and fun fabrics or paint colors: Enhance their original wit by adding your own. Bright hues look equally great on rugs, textiles, and accessories, too.

Use your imagination. New paint and fabric are great ways to get creative with vintage pieces, but you can go further. Repurpose things and combine them in unexpected ways. With a new color and custom cushion, a twin-size headboard became a foyer bench in Duck's Nest, and a set of wicker fish and an old fishing rod, newly wired together, became a chandelier.

MAKE IT PRACTICAL

A patinaed surface is your best friend. If you find a great-looking vintage piece with decades of use behind it, you're in luck. You know it's aged gracefully, even with years of wear and tear, so you can rest assured it'll only get better. (Bonus: Contrast between older, rougher textures and sleeker contemporary ones looks great.)

Always sit in vintage seating before you buy. A lot of antique sofas, chairs, stools, and chaises are smaller and lower slung than you're used to. Replacing the seat cushions with new ones—perhaps with thicker, stronger, and more supportive foam or another filling—can raise the height and ensure your comfort.

Can't find what you need? Have it made. An antique or vintage item can serve as inspiration, even when you don't buy it for your home. If you see something you like, but it's the wrong size or material, commission a custom piece to echo it instead. That's what I did for a shadow box–style bamboo coffee table and nesting bamboo end tables at Duck's Nest.

OPPOSITE AND PREVIOUS PAGES: Nearly every stick of furniture in this house is vintage, and the owner and I searched near and far to find them. These older items, with their sense of age, patina, and quirk, make the house's interiors feel like they were collected over the course of years and years, maybe even generations.

position. The bright yellows, blues, and greens of its stained-glass windows and doors, for instance—from which I borrowed the redesign's cheerful new color palette—felt pulled from the sunset, the water, and the lush surrounding gardens.

There's a delightful sense of relaxation here, too, a casual, fun element that stems from the charms of the Victorian architecture. We spun this into the atmosphere throughout, selecting cane, wicker, and rattan furniture that always feels at home on the coast but especially here. We painted most of the wooden walls and ceilings a sparkling, low-maintenance white, the best way to reflect the sunny highlights on the water outside.

The exterior and much of the historic interior architecture had such a whimsical and inviting Old Florida feeling to them that we wanted to make sure the decoration was just as fun and welcoming, especially since the owners would use this as a guesthouse and entertaining space. We landed on something of a hip vintage vibe perfect for parties, and the owners and I had a ton of fun scouring South Florida and well beyond for fabulous finds.

Eventually, things got to the point where I said, "We need to have a record player! We've got to have vinyl." And we got both. To be honest, I was one step away from doing macramé plant holders and glass beads in the doors.

To ensure the house remains as sophisticated as it is swinging, I stopped short of taking those final playful steps. But I still can't help but smile when I see Duck's Nest in its re-feathered state. I know the owners—and their guests—feel the same.

OPPOSITE, PREVIOUS, AND FOLLOWING PAGES: I borrowed my turquoise-blue, lime-green, and lemon-yellow palette from the colors of the stained glass in some of the house's original doors and windows. Clean white walls, floors, and ceilings let the saturated hues of the colorful upholstery and painted pieces really pop.

ABOVE AND OPPOSITE: Tucked away off the living room's back seating nook and accessed through a bamboo door, the setting of the bar led me to some swank, speakeasy-style decoration. I chose a relatively dark color for the walls and had the wide-plank wood floors painted in a geometric pattern. In a home designed for entertaining, I couldn't imagine a better spot. Could you?

ABOVE, OPPOSITE, AND FOLLOWING PAGES: As you might be able to tell, the whole scheme for the kitchen came from a set of blue-and-white-striped Cornishware, which the homeowner and I found at one of our favorite local vintage shops. Even though we both loved it, it took some convincing to get her to go along with this bold scheme, which includes white-painted floors, tiled counters and backsplash, and a custom checked wallpaper for the ceiling and fabric for the sink skirt.
PREVIOUS PAGES: If you can't find the perfect light fixture, make your own. I found these woven fish in Paris and the fishing pole at a vintage shop in Florida. Then I took it all to the lamp shop Edgar-Reeves Lighting in Atlanta and got it assembled and wired—and voilà!

Designing with
PLAYFUL COLOR

Blend and balance. Combine colors that are next to each other on the color wheel with an accent hue opposite them. Here, the red-pink flowers pop against the mix of turquoise-y greens and blues. The white walls, ceilings, and floors at Duck's Nest beautifully set off all the brightness.

Go big—and little, too. You can use color in ways large and small and to equally aesthetically pleasing effect. Here, broad swaths of tone make a statement on the upholstery and in the rugs, but painting just the railing of an otherwise neutral staircase can be just as impactful, as can choosing pillows, lampshades, and tabletop items in bold hues.

Know your limits. A room looks best when the number of main colors used is kept to three (though you can add a small additional accent hue or two). This allows even the most colorful spaces to look calm and never too busy. I love color almost more than anyone, but even I find that I only want to take it so far.

The brighter the better. Waterfront houses enjoy lots of sun, and daylight is lovely, but it can make subtle colors look washed out and contrasts disappear. That's why bright hues are best by the beach. (They keep things nice at night, too, when water views fade to black.)

Think saturated more than dark. Colors can look rich and bright without being dark. Navy blues, maroons, forest greens, and blacks tend to show every grain of sand and speck of dust—and waterfront houses tend to attract a fair bit of both. Think about bold yellows, lime and kelly greens, royal and sky blues, turquoises, and corals instead.

Resist the fade. Strong sun can quickly cause many colorful textiles and rugs, and even some paint, to lose its color. On the water, and with big windows, it's especially important to find fade-resistant fabrics and other materials. Often, this means using so-called "performance" textiles and other indoor-outdoor items. But don't worry, these days, outdoor fabrics have just as lovely a hand feel as indoor ones.

Wicker, cane, and bamboo furniture work together with a rag rug and simple woven blinds to lend the living room a decidedly relaxed, casual air. We kept most of the furniture low-slung to keep views to the water open.

ABOVE AND OPPOSITE: The fun continues in a part of the house that was an addition to the original, but until this renovation had been more of a screened porch. Now enclosed and air-conditioned, it serves a bevy of uses, which I delineated with a few groupings of furniture, one of which can be used as a breakfast room or games area set between the fireplace on one side and a bamboo credenza on the other.

A generously sized curved sofa and two sets of paired vintage stick-wicker chairs—newly painted white—define the seating area in the former porch. The crown molding recalls the scalloped shapes of the house's exterior, a motif repeated in the woven wicker pendant light.

ABOVE, OPPOSITE, AND PREVIOUS PAGES: Because its owners—who live primarily in an adjacent property—use Duck's Nest for visitors and party space, every bedroom in it is a guest room. That freed us up to have plenty of fun. I combined patterns big and small and mixed vintage and antique items with those designed to look fabulously old-fashioned, like café curtains with pom-pom edging.

Each of the bedrooms in the house got its own color, and I love the coral hue here, as well as the seashell lamps we had made. There's a bulb under the shade and in the shell, so the base can glow at night. FOLLOWING PAGES: Glass front doors let you look right through the house to the Intracoastal Waterway beyond the backyard.

Jolly Harbour

on't let the pristine blue-and-white beauty of this house fool you. Despite the elegant, at times even delicate, appearance of its interiors, this vacation home on the Caribbean island of Antigua is absolutely indestructible. Its owners conceived it as an over-flow guesthouse—a place to put up extra company when they had more visitors than could comfortably sleep at their main property—and they imagined they would also rent it out as a holiday home. That meant they wouldn't always know exactly who was staying here, and they wouldn't have great visibility on all that went on within its walls, either. They wanted the place to be as pretty as the lovely azure- and cerulean-blue Jolly Harbour it overlooked. But it needed to be able to take a beating, too.

How to achieve both goals at once? A regal palette of royal blue and bright white patterns and solids, warmed up by natural, neutral tones and woven tex-tures, nearly all of it rendered in outdoor fabrics and other rugged materials. The textiles and carpets you see here are indoor-outdoor—made to be water resistant, easy to clean, and able to withstand heavy use.

OPPOSITE AND FOLLOWING PAGES: A blue-and-white living room looks anything but basic when you mix artisanal hand block prints, stripes, and batiks, then add textured natural elements. PREVIOUS PAGES: Waterfront settings don't get any better than this one overlooking Antigua's Jolly Harbour.

ABOVE AND OPPOSITE: The wave pattern of the kitchen's mosaic-tile backsplash became one of the homeowners' favorite design elements. Since lower cabinets always get more wear and tear, we left these unpainted, which is better for avoiding chips and scratches. The upper ones got a coat of white paint, however, which helps make the blue backsplash pop.

ABOVE: As far as I'm concerned, you can never have too much blue, and this bookshelf proves my point. OPPOSITE: The media room's several shades of navy blend together beautifully, even though they don't quite match.

Designing a
GUESTHOUSE PRIMARY SUITE

MAKE IT PRETTY

Decorate for everyone. Because you don't know who exactly will use the room, try to design it to have universal appeal, making it neither too feminine nor too masculine. Blue is the world's favorite color, so it is always well received.

Think big with the bed. One place you can make more of a style statement? The bed. I love a four-poster or canopy in a guesthouse's primary suite—and your visitors will, too. It should always be a king. No one wants to sleep in a smaller bed, especially on vacation.

Raise the bar on luxury and comfort. The primary suite in a guesthouse will be the first to be filled, so it will have the most frequent visitors and often more important ones. While you can cut some corners in the other bedrooms, increase your spend on quality fabrics and accessories here to make it feel like a private haven—a vacation within a vacation house.

MAKE IT PRACTICAL

Storage matters. Guests come with suitcases—oftentimes large ones. The primary bedroom will have the largest closet and should have at least two luggage racks, but I also like to put a bench or stools at the foot of the bed for luggage. Be sure to use fabrics that are easy to clean (and consider adding a fun jolt of color to closet walls, even if the bedroom has white ones).

A place apart. Often smaller than a main residence, a property's guesthouse may only have one living area. For that reason, I always like to design some seating into the primary bedroom of a guesthouse. Here, the room's covered porch serves as a private sitting and dining area where a couple can take a break from a larger crowd.

Screen time. I almost always put a TV in the primary suite of a guesthouse, even though I avoid them in the rest of the guest rooms. Like a seating area, it helps the main bedroom feel like more of a sanctuary, and it gives a place for visitors to retreat. I like to put a remote control on each bedside table, with a laminated channel card. Make sure to mount the TV high enough for clear views from the bed.

A seating area off the primary suite provides a perfect place for morning coffee and reading away from house guests or a sweet place to escape any time of day.

Not so long ago, trying to design an entire interior with these materials would have been very limiting. But these tougher-than-tough, high-quality performance textiles now come in all the colorways, prints, and textures you can imagine. And, most importantly, they feel just as pleasant to touch as indoor fabrics.

All the jute-, sisal-, and seagrass-style rugs here are polypropylene, able to be taken outside, hosed down, and dried in the sun as soon as they get dirty. Even the curtains and blinds are made of outdoor fabrics, so they are washable, wrinkle-resistant, and won't fade easily in the sun. And the tile floors throughout are incredibly low-maintenance, too.

To my mind, there's little better than a blue-and-white interior by the water. And I knew the owners of this house agreed with me. I'd done another island home for them in a similar palette, and they'd loved it. Now, they'd purchased a property with spectacular bay views and room after room that opened to the water or the pool through large windows and doors. Caribbean breezes blew through the house, usually—but not always—gently, and the sound of lapping water could be heard nearly everywhere you went.

The blue colors and the mix of botanical and artisanal prints and patterns I layered here, including ikats and hand blocking, help bring the outdoors in. So does the combination of natural materials, many of them left in an untreated state—or at least left with the appearance of natural materials in an untreated state.

OPPOSITE: The turned posts of the four-poster bed provide a great-looking echo of the silhouette of the bedside chests. FOLLOWING PAGES: I confess, I'm a pillow girl. Is ten too many for this bed? Maybe . . . but sue me. It just makes it look so welcoming.

Simple can be sensationally stunning. When you're working with a stellar view like this, decoration without distraction is my mantra.

The simple, traditional architecture of each room—clad in ivory-hued limestone floors, whitewashed wood ceilings, and white-painted plaster walls—and the overarching blue-and-white color scheme created enough of a blank canvas that I could really play with pattern in these interiors. Blues blend so well that they help different prints work well together, too. And that's something very useful in a house that's going to get a lot of use. Bolder, complex patterns tend to hide stains and dirt. Blemishes blend in, or at least the eye is so distracted by everything else going on, any imperfections all but disappear.

And there's plenty going on here. Some of the homeowners' favorite moments—and mine, too—are the boldest: the wave pattern of the kitchen's sapphire and turquoise mosaic backsplash; the den's palm-print curtains and deep midnight-blue velvet sleeper sofa; the layers of patterns used in the super-soft cotton bedding; and the statement-making plaster, woven, string-wrapped, and beaded pendant lamps and chandeliers in nearly every room. What's not to love?

If you live by the water, the amount of outdoor seating you have should always match the number of bedrooms, so that everyone staying in the house has a place to sit or lounge outside.

Designing for
OUTDOOR DINING

MAKE IT PRETTY

Build from the bottom up. For a soft, finished look, use a heavy felt liner underneath thinner tablecloths. Then layer on texture with woven placemats, color with printed and solid napkins, and shimmer with dishes and drinkware. Napkin rings, salt and pepper shakers, and hurricane lanterns make things feel more fun.

Go beyond the table. The vacation vibe of waterfront houses means meals start early and go late. Your decoration can encourage this and make it more pleasurable. Add interesting stools and ottomans so people can put their feet up or place a drink down. Offer baskets with throw blankets coordinated to your decorating so friends can stay outside on cool evenings.

Keep an eye on the view. If you have impressive waterfront vistas—and I hope you do—your decorating will probably take a backseat. This is especially true at sunset. Arrange seating and other furniture to maximize everyone's enjoyment of the scenery, and pull your colors and textures from the natural surroundings.

MAKE IT PRACTICAL

Plastic makes perfect. Especially with all those bare feet and open-toed shoes around, you want to do away with fears about breakage. Trade china and glass for melamine and plastic. There are so many beautiful sets of dishware and drinkware available in these materials, plus all the serving pieces you could need when entertaining a crowd.

See the light. Use plenty of sconces plus recessed and monopoint lights to evenly illuminate your table, your guests, and any serving or drinks areas. I'm also a fan of fans in outdoor spaces. They create a cooling breeze when there isn't a natural one, and they can reduce the presence of insects. (Remember to keep lights five feet away from fans, or they'll create a strobe effect.)

Comfort is king. Long, lingering meals make it especially important to have comfortable dining chairs. You want seat cushions thick enough to sit in for hours—at least three inches of open-cell foam, which lets water flow through and dries quickly. And, if you have room, armchairs are more pleasant than side chairs.

OPPOSITE AND FOLLOWING PAGES: This house was designed for outdoor living and entertaining—so much so that it doesn't even have a real indoor dining area.

Atlantic Beach

*t*he owner of this house in the North Florida town of Atlantic Beach first fell for it because of its impressive oceanfront setting and the relatively modest charms of its original 1920s architecture. She loved that old beach-house feeling and wanted to carry the atmosphere created by the white-painted wood walls, cedar-shake exterior, and cozy floor plan into the new interiors of the home, as well as those of a more recently built guesthouse.

With my designer-husband, Jim, imagining the interior architecture, and me developing the decorating scheme, we landed on a shared goal: to preserve as much of the hundred-year-old waterfront building and its character-rich details as we possibly could. But unfortunately, the powers that be had other ideas. The city decided the structure was too unstable for us to proceed, and it had to be torn down. We were all heartbroken. But we regrouped and then worked with architect James Dupree to create a new house with all the charms of the original—plus the structural innovations and hurricane security of twenty-first-century building technology.

Now, both outside and in, the house celebrates the past while living in the present and looking not only toward the future but out at its utterly sensational ocean view.

Beyond telling me about her desire for a home inspired by that 1920s Florida beach-house style and spirit, the owner largely gave me carte blanche. But I knew

OPPOSITE AND FOLLOWING PAGES: The foyer sets the tone for what follows at this North Florida home. Textured wood walls, detailed millwork, natural materials, and the owner's favorite shades of robin's-egg blue make their way from room to room. PREVIOUS PAGES: Although newly built, the house echoes the 1920s beachfront style of the region.

We brought in as much charming, old-fashioned architecture as we could to create an Old Florida feeling.

a few things about her and how she and her three grown sons, who'd be visiting with friends and significant others, would use the house, which would be a second home for weekends and holidays.

First off, they're an active family, who love to entertain both indoors and out. Cue the French doors, outdoor living areas, patios, porches, pool, firepit, and putting green.

I also knew she wanted the place to be easy to maintain but pretty, too, and that it had to be flexible enough to feel comfortable for twenty guests or just for her and a friend. I additionally gathered that it should reflect her own personal style, which is classic and tailored but feminine. She dresses mostly in solids with just one colorful accessory.

The scheme we came up with gave her just what she wanted and even more. She got that old-fashioned Florida beach-house feel from the textured white wood walls, coffered ceilings, and other millwork details Jim designed, plus the wicker, rattan, and vintage furniture I selected. Fresh florals and paisleys like those in the living room are timeless choices by the water, as are the mosaic floors, freestanding tub, and shutters in the primary suite's bath.

OPPOSITE AND FOLLOWING PAGES: Creating multiple intimate seating areas in a large living room makes it work as well for a big party as it does for a small gathering. The mix of floral, paisley, and woodblock prints feels classic by the coast, as do the beadboard walls, driftwood hues, jute carpet, nautical-feeling light fixtures, and pastel painting by Shawn Dulaney.

The blue-and-white palette couldn't be beachier. We wove the owner's beloved robin's-egg blue throughout the house. In the kitchen, where the hue covers both walls and cabinets, the blue is at its most saturated; elsewhere, it's just an accent, sometimes bright, usually more muted. Pretty as it all is, we used low-maintenance performance fabrics or laminated textiles as much as possible to make upkeep a breeze, and I picked pieces with textures and finishes that would survive any wear and tear as beautiful patina.

The fact that the property is divided into a three-bedroom main house and a three-bedroom guesthouse means that there's plenty of room for everyone, but no individual space seems too big. And to ensure that it felt cozy even when the owner was by herself or with a very small group, we turned one of the main house's upstairs bedrooms into a casual sitting area with its own porch—a great complement to the larger, more formal living room below.

For her and her family, this oceanfront property is now an old-meets-new retreat that feels like their own private resort, whatever the size of the group they're with.

As lovely as this octagonal dining room is, it's easy to keep clean. Choosing performance fabrics for most of the textiles and opting to keep the floor rug-free make that possible. Note how the Giacometti-style plaster chandelier echoes the forms of the palms outside the French doors.

For the owner of this house, there was no amount of robin's-egg blue that could be too much. Still, it was important to balance it with warmer tones and textures. FOLLOWING PAGES: The upstairs seating area and porch provide a spot for the homeowner to relax when she has the house to herself and doesn't need the space of the main living room.

Designing a
STATEMENT STAIRCASE

MAKE IT PRETTY

Layer on texture and tone. Here, smooth millwork frames relatively rough inset wall panels of painted cypress, and wool carpet with a slightly distressed texture covers bleached-oak floors. Pairing a stained banister with painted balustrades and newel posts provides additional, albeit light, contrast.

Add visual interest with coastal details. Every surface is an opportunity for ornament. Jim designed the Vitruvian scroll detail for the skirtboards to mimic the look of waves, while the urn on the newel nods to the house's classical style. The runner I selected has a beachy look that complements the ocean outside.

Let in the light. Whenever possible, allow windows and skylights to flood steps with sunlight. The warmth and illumination make for a welcoming scene and draw attention upward. I also like to line a stair with wall sconces, adding a hanging lamp above and maybe even downlights on each step. Multiple light sources create an even glow.

MAKE IT PRACTICAL

Comfort is always key. A carpet and pad underfoot make a staircase easier on feet and knees, and they muffle sound, too, which lets late risers keep sleeping. I'm a big believer in the importance of how a handrail feels when you're using it—getting it perfectly smooth requires lots of sanding and layers of paint or stain.

Hide wear and tear with pattern. This wool rug's mottled motif makes most marks left by muddy feet and shoes blend right in, and the material is easy to have cleaned. The variegated, faux-driftwood finish of the textured wall panels, meanwhile, disguises stray sticky fingerprints. (Solids show much more dirt.)

Pale colors disguise sand and dust. Lighter hues won't actually keep your house clean, but they will help make it look like it is—even if conventional wisdom used to be that darker shades were easier to maintain. At the beach, nothing hides sand and dust better than, well, the colors of sand and dust. Camouflage is your friend!

OPPOSITE: Every detail of the staircase subtly suggests the 1920s Florida style the owner wanted.
FOLLOWING PAGES: Diverse textures enliven the relatively monochromatic palette of this guest room.

ABOVE AND OPPOSITE: An array of materials and subtle patterns can be found in
the primary bedroom, where a light lavender hue casts a feminine glow.
PREVIOUS PAGES: Mosaic tiles, a freestanding tub, and wooden shutters combine
to create a vintage-modern atmosphere in the primary bathroom.

For an active family that enjoys spending time together, creating a home that encourages easy indoor-outdoor living was key. This porch is just one of several places where they can gather alfresco to enjoy each other's company. The views aren't half bad either.

Thin frames and the lattice weave of rope-wrapped teak furniture make for a lighter-than-air look. The pieces nicely recall the spacing between the railing balustrades and keep the focus firmly on the view.

Villa Capri

t his cliffside house overlooking an aquamarine bay in Antigua represents a departure from its owners' usual design aesthetic—and my own, too. It's the third Caribbean home we've collaborated on together, following their residences in Puerto Rico, where we created bright, cheerful schemes awash in various vibrant shades. That's a look I always love by the water, especially in the tropics, but here, the homeowners wanted something quite different.

They asked me to use an entirely neutral but still very warm palette, without any real color. I was surprised at first, but then I realized that this would allow the house's stunning blue and green views to really, well, stun—and without having to compete with the decorating at all. The relatively quiet, monochromatic interior concept would also open up a world of possibilities for layering rich, island-appropriate textures, both rustic and refined. These would keep the consistent color palette visually interesting, inviting, and even fun.

And fun was a very important part of the equation here. That's because the owners wanted this house—in contrast to their primary residence—to feel like a true vacation. They saw it as a place where they, and their friends and family, could retreat, relax, rejuvenate, and just have a good time.

Fun was also key because of the island's overall spirit of joy, which I encountered whenever I met anyone who called Antigua home. Everyone I met just loved living here. Young or old, rich or poor, they seemed to appreciate that they got to wake up

OPPOSITE: When you're designing with a palette of neutrally hued, natural materials, there's (almost) no such thing as too much texture. PREVIOUS PAGES: Both outdoors and in, I used a neutral color palette that didn't even try to compete with the scene-stealing Caribbean views.

Designing a
DINING ROOM

Frame views with curtains. In an oceanfront island house's dining room, the vista out the window is always the focal point. Curtains—even solid-colored sheers like these—highlight the beauty of what's outside. And, at night, even when it's dark, with the windows or doors open, they billow beautifully in the breeze.

Open means inviting. The furniture in this room, though large, has a certain lightness that creates a welcoming sense of space. The open fretwork on the back of the tall armchairs at the table, the thin top and narrow legs of the table itself, and the coco beads of the tiered chandelier all have an airy feeling, letting those island breezes blow through.

Give the tablescape a sense of place. Use tropical flowers and greenery for centerpieces and other botanical arrangements around a dining room. Fruit from the area, lovingly arranged in an artisanal glass bowl, also makes for an appropriately appetizing, not to mention edible, accent. If the climate is right, don't forget coconuts and conch shells, too.

Reconsider the rug. In a casual island house like this—or really any home by the water where sand, mud, and wet feet will be impossible to keep out—I like a bare floor under the table. This also keeps you from having to save a carpet from red wine, barbecue sauce, or oil stains. It just means less to clean, and I'm always all for that. (We laminated the ikat fabric on the dining chairs for the same reason.)

More paint means less maintenance. Painted surfaces are easier to care for because they don't develop drink rings and scratches like stained or untreated wood. Here, I used painted chairs and a painted dining table. To add texture, I like to vary the finishes of the paint from matte and distressed to high-gloss and sleek.

The tall and short of candles. When you want to enjoy a waterfront meal with the dining room's doors and windows open so you can let the breeze in, it's always a good idea to use hurricane lamps that are on the higher side. That helps prevent candles from blowing out (and you from having to relight them).

OPPOSITE: The homeowner found the vintage suzani that I then had framed and hung as artwork in the dining room. PREVIOUS PAGES: Wooden ceilings, sisal rugs, and a richly textured mix of woven materials lend the living room warmth.

Because stained finishes don't chip, staining lower cabinets—even if you have the upper ones painted—keeps your kitchen looking newer longer.

in paradise every day, and that gave them a sense of happiness I've encountered in few other destinations. I wanted this house to do the same for its owners.

I set about weaving together a scheme that pulled from the organic textures of the island's landscapes and from its traditional architecture. Naturally, that meant selecting furnishings that made the most of woven materials, including rope and string, cane and wicker, and sisal, abaca, and grass cloth. These pieces occupy rooms with architectural finishes that remain the same from one space to the next, the better to maintain a consistent atmosphere and keep the emphasis on the views. Traditional Caribbean wood ceilings got a driftwood-colored stain, like much of the furniture below them, and a decorative painter washed the walls with layer upon layer of a watered-down cream hue to add depth and a bit of a sense of age. The floor's large tiles of limestone feel of a piece with the property's dramatic coral stone exterior staircase, which connects the house to a private beach.

I know what you're wondering. With all that uniformity and overall neutral palette, how did I keep things interesting and fun from one room to the next?

OPPOSITE: I painted the kitchen's upper cabinets to break up the wood tones of the ceiling and lower cabinetry. PREVIOUS PAGES: A simply styled, monumental eighteenth-century bookcase creates an alternate focal point to the living room's wall of windows.

The answer lies, first and foremost, in the addition of just the right amount of variation: The pattern of the neutral wool carpets changes oh-so subtly among the spaces; the exact weave on seating and lighting is also never identical. The same materials, meanwhile, appear again and again in different forms, used in new, often surprising, ways. Rope creates a basketweave in the living room's chunky seating, then wraps an elegantly lithe four-poster bed in a guest room. The capiz shells of the primary suite's tiered chandelier return in the kitchen, where I used them in a most novel way: They form a backsplash that shimmers and reflects light like the sparkling sea.

Batik, ikat, paisley, and block prints, all still in warm neutrals, add additional accents. They, too, are all different, but they remain connected, thanks to their neutral colorways and the sense of traditional, handmade artisanship that defines the aesthetic of each.

I did allow myself one departure from the neutral palette—a subtle pink, inspired by the color inside the conch shells that dot the beach here. That accent hue makes a singular statement in the large paisley used for all the upholstery and the floor-to-ceiling curtains in the library. It even tints the grass cloth covering the coffee table. The whole room emits a rosy glow that casts everyone who enters in a good light.

Not long after the project was finished, the owners sent me a note saying they've never been as happy as they are in this home. And they've had a lot of houses! It seems that they, too, discovered the joy of waking up in paradise.

I broke the house's all-neutral-all-the-time scheme ever so slightly in the library.
Here, a subtle range of rose hues—inspired by the colors inside a conch shell—sits
well with the warm wood paneling and the woven light fixture and blinds.

ABOVE: A little nook formed by the turn in the stairs creates an easy excuse for a decorative vignette. OPPOSITE: The primary bedroom is mostly done in solids, apart from the small pattern used for the curtains and the Indian block prints on the bed.

It's kids who more often than not end up in a twin bedroom, and even they deserve an amazing view, if you can spare it. This house, thankfully, has no shortage of vistas— or bedrooms.

People always ask me how high to hang curtains—and the answer is that it really depends on your space. Here, I went with halfway between the top of the glass doors and the wood ceiling because it felt like just enough but not too much fabric.

Designing a
GUEST BEDROOM

MAKE IT PRETTY

Focus on bedding. I always use four sleeping pillows, then a few additional euro and decorative pillows. Each is an opportunity to introduce complementary patterns, textures, and colors. I like a blanket or quilt at the foot of the bed, which is another place for prints. In warm-weather waterfront locations, cotton is best, and you can skip the duvet.

Layering sunlight control. Another location to add pretty style? Window treatments—and you'll want plenty of them. Best is some combination of blackout and sheers, whether two curtains, two shades (Roman or roll), or a curtain and a shade. If guests like to wake with the sun, they can always leave the blackouts open, but people usually want the sheers for privacy.

Decorate more prettily than personally. Family photos and mementos and out-there art have their place, but it's not here. Hospitable touches such as a lovely carafe of water, a vase of flowers, some current magazines, and even a chocolate on the pillow show your guests you care.

MAKE IT PRACTICAL

Hang it all out. In a waterfront house, you can never have too many hooks for drying towels, bathing suits, or that pair of capris you didn't mean to get wet when you went for a walk on the beach. This is especially true in guest rooms, since visitors may not have (or want) access to your washing machine and dryer. The backs of doors, bathroom walls, and closets are all great places to hide them.

Less is more. I like to use just a few pieces of furniture—the minimal amount, really—in guest rooms. It just makes it easier for your visitors to find their way around what will be an unfamiliar space, minimizing the risk of bumps in the night. It also means there's less to maintain and keep free of sand and dirt.

Ensure sound sleep. Sleep in your guest suites from time to time to make sure bedrooms and bathrooms are at their best. Only by living as your guests will can you know that everything is in working order. (Visitors won't always feel comfortable telling you something isn't quite right.)

In a house with high vaulted ceilings like these, four-poster and canopy-style beds are a must. The same is true of eye-catching, large-scale pendant light fixtures and chandeliers.

ABOVE, OPPOSITE, AND FOLLOWING PAGES: Every time I step outside this house—or even just look out a window—I'm reminded of why we kept things neutral inside. I've never second-guessed the decision to let nature have exclusive rights to the bright Caribbean palette here.

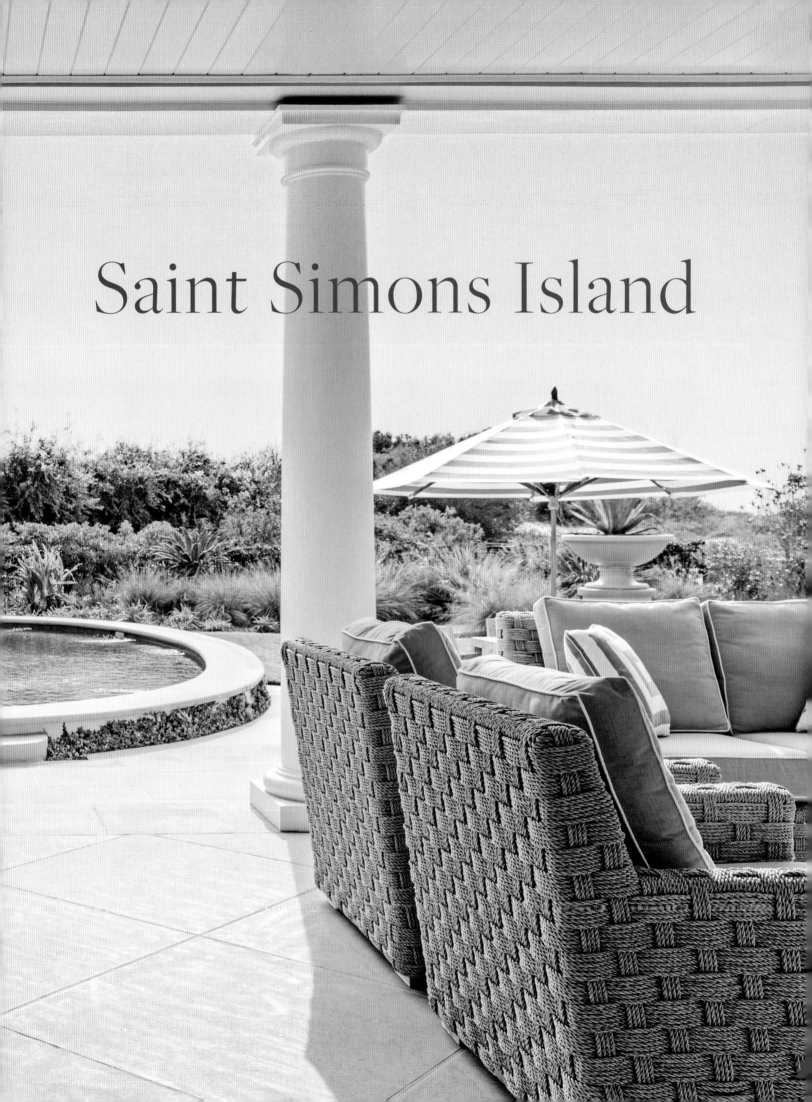

Saint Simons Island

n ot only does this newly built, classically styled home on Saint Simons Island, just off the Georgia coast, owe its blue-green color palette, seaside accessories, and laid-back but sophisticated style to its waterfront position, it also has that setting to thank for its entire two-story plan, too. Architect George Hopkins Jr. based his overarching scheme on the particular way this house relates to the water.

Because rolling sand dunes filled with foliage separate properties here from the beach and the ocean beyond, to maximize water views, George designed the owner's new home as a so-called "upside-down house." That means all of its main public and entertaining spaces, and even some of its most-used private ones, too, sit on the second floor. This configuration enables these rooms' large expanses of windows, glass doors, and porches to provide the most impressive panoramic vistas. There's nothing but dunes and sea as far as the eye can see.

The plan made perfect sense for the owner—a stylish woman who loves spending time connected to nature. By day, you'll find her riding her bike and playing golf and tennis before she slips into a little cocktail dress to entertain at home. Whether held indoors or out, her parties always have great southern charm. The minute I met her, I knew she'd bring excellent taste to the table and plenty of trust in my aesthetic and vision. A designer's dream!

As for the architect's vision for this upside-down house, it made complete sense to me, too, both because it would take the best advantage of the property's

OPPOSITE: Architect George Hopkins designed the entry of this house in coastal Georgia to feel like a glass-enclosed porch. PREVIOUS PAGES: The glass allows you to see to the back of the house, where a patio and serene oval-shaped pool beckon.

Using vintage items throughout
this house appealed to its antique-
collecting owner's love of pieces
that have history and patina.

views *and* because it connected well to the antique-collecting owner's desire for a house that would bridge the formal and the casual, the traditional and modern. Just the kind of combo I like.

We decided to reserve most of the more elevated and classical furnishings for the entertaining-ready upper story, which held an open living room, dining area, and kitchen, plus the primary suite and a home office that doubled as a private sitting room. I then designed the ground level—featuring three guest bedrooms, plus a family room with a hidden bar and pair of games tables—to feel more relaxed. Of course, because I'm me, we mixed things up a bit both upstairs and down to keep the formal from feeling fussy and the relaxed from feeling too casual.

The owner's love of antique furniture, plus vintage crystal, china, silver, and table linens—and her impressive collections of heirlooms of all of these—made it a particular joy to imagine the elevated upstairs settings. Pulling beautiful tones of pale blue, light aqua, fern green, and sunny yellows from the coastal surroundings, and treating the windows to sheer curtains that would frame the views, I set about collecting evermore fabulous antiques for her, searching everywhere from

OPPOSITE AND PREVIOUS PAGES: Antiques including a large Dutch cabinet, now used to house the TV, and casual stick-wicker chairs, found in Palm Beach, add personality to the living room. The painting is by Wellon Bridgers.

A consistent color palette of
blue and green seafoam hues
connects everything together in
the open living and dining area.

Palm Beach, Florida, to Parma, Italy, with stops in the English countryside and Paris in between. I found pieces with great character and history, plus the sort of rich patina the homeowner was so attuned to.

Just some of the highlights? The entryway's English center table with a patinated copper top; the powder room's bamboo-pine vanity from the Cotswolds, with its original marble counter; and the living room's ornately inlaid nineteenth-century Italian bombé chest of drawers. Delicately paned glass-and-wood fretwork doors by Palm Beach architect John Volk front the family room's bar, and, in the living room, I gathered stick-wicker chairs, the homeowner's gilded mirror, and a large eighteenth-century Dutch cabinet, repurposed here to conceal a television.

Antiques and other one-of-a-kind items were so important in this house because the owner didn't want things to feel typical or predictable, and the design here proves itself anything but. Still, even though the house is upside down—and dotted with wonderfully unique antique and vintage finds whose charms add a definite bit of quirk—there's nothing topsy-turvy about this home. It's the picture of subtle seaside sophistication.

A gilded mirror from the homeowner's existing collection of one-of-a-kind,
well-selected antiques hangs in the dining area. I balanced its potential formality
with the playful pattern and skirting on the upholstered chairs.

Designing a
POWDER ROOM

MAKE IT PRETTY

Well-clad walls. A powder room provides the perfect place to go big and bold with wallpaper. Even the highest impact of patterns won't overwhelm in a relatively small space. Since this room was on the larger side, we could go with a very large print depicting tropical greenery over a bamboo cane background.

Make old new. Antiques lend personality to any space, powder rooms included. This vintage pine washstand had a high backsplash with an upper shelf that was all original. That protects the wallpaper from any water that may escape the sink.

Glow up. Whether sconces like the ones here or pendants hung from the ceiling, powder room lighting can serve not just as a source of illumination but also as a glittering decorating touch that completes a space. Think of it as the piece of shimmering jewelry you add to an outfit just before you leave the house.

MAKE IT PRACTICAL

Count on counter space. When you have room for it, as we did here, giving guests enough surface area to put down a handbag and phone is a dream in a powder room. This vanity's two tiers allow for decorative touches and soaps up top, leaving space below for guests' items.

For on the floor. These days, you can have your wooden floors treated to become all but impermeable to spills and moisture, making them a safe choice even in a powder room. Extending this home's oak flooring from the living area into this space also allows for a seamless visual transition.

Mirror, mirror. Every powder room, no matter how small, must have a mirror—the bigger the better, even in the teeniest spaces. Guests need to see themselves, a wallpapered wall needs to have something simple on it, and you'll want to bounce light around as much as possible to make the space seem bigger.

Positioned just off the main living and dining area, this powder room continues the blue-green palette of that space but trades quiet white walls for this tropically patterned wallpaper. That sort of bold move is easy to get away with in a small space like this one.

Designing a
BACK KITCHEN

MAKE IT PRETTY

Accessories matter. It's a major trend today to build a back kitchen, also called a scullery, to let the front kitchen be the showpiece your guests see, leaving this one to be harder working. But it's still nice to show it some love: Shells and sea glass collected by the owner do just that here.

Surfaces shine. Classic materials like those you might find in a working kitchen in a grand Gilded Age home keep things great-looking in this house's scullery. I used white paint for the lower cabinets and then topped them with polished Calacatta Caldia marble counters. From there, I added a big farmhouse sink and artisanally glazed white zellige tile all the way up the walls.

Treat windows well. My love of café curtains knows absolutely no limits, as anyone who knows me will tell you. They let in just enough light to keep things bright, they provide you with just enough privacy, and they're just so charming. They work wonders in this room.

MAKE IT PRACTICAL

Space matters. No one wants to take square footage away from the "show kitchen" up front, which guests will see, but there's no overstating how important prep space is, to say nothing of having extra room to hold mess. I rearranged this back kitchen to get it to work harder and hold more appliances.

Let there be light. That rearranging also let me get a window into the room, which helps it feel open. Yes, this is a hardworking space, but it's also designed for everyday use by the homeowner, and it should be pleasant to work in.

Make access easy. Open shelving is pretty in a main kitchen, but it can be impractical because it's hard to keep neat. It's perfect in a back kitchen, however, because no one has to see it! And it sure makes it easier to grab what you need when you need it. (I couldn't resist keeping these pretty, though, doing them in cerused oak with hammered-bronze straps.)

OPPOSITE: Having a back kitchen, also called a scullery, helps conceal prep work and messy cooking. PREVIOUS PAGES: Thanks to that scullery, this main kitchen, featuring a large island and pewter-hued hood, gets to shine as a showpiece.

ABOVE: Patterned concrete tiles add visual surprise to the stairs. OPPOSITE: A barnacle-encrusted bust from the owner's collection tops a console table. PREVIOUS PAGES: I kept things simple in the primary bedroom, using the same pattern for the curtains and wall covering, and sticking to that print's two-color palette throughout.

ABOVE, OPPOSITE, AND PREVIOUS PAGES: The ground-floor family room owes its casual
atmosphere to its comfy sectional and wicker chairs set at a pair of games tables. When I found
the vintage glass-and-wood fretwork doors, I knew they'd add sparkle to the bar here.

The homeowner asked me to make her office more than just a workspace. She wanted a spot where she'd be comfortable relaxing with a book or talking on the phone when she didn't have guests who could help her fill the larger living area. With this cozy, sunny little sitting room, we gave her just that.

In this, the largest of the
house's three guest rooms,
we gave a vintage bed from
the owner's collection new life
by reupholstering it in a
playful print. I coordinated
the other patterns in the
room to the bed by picking
fabrics in different scales but
the same colorway.

I always like to give each guest room in a house its own color. Doing so provides some unique personality–plus, it's nice to be able to refer to the room by its hue, to help visitors find their space.

ABOVE: The walled garden—designed by landscape designer Jeremy Smearman—provides ample opportunity for outdoor relaxation. OPPOSITE: On the covered porch, I repeated the blue-green color of the garden gate's trim for the cabana-striped seat cushions and the tabletop pieces.

Naples Bay

i t's always a joy to collaborate with homeowners who come to the table with a strong sense of aesthetic direction and great taste, too. The empty-nester couple who asked me to help them with this house certainly had both. They'd bought a large piece of property with wide water frontage on Naples Bay, on Florida's western coast, and worked with architect John Cooney and builder Joe Beauchamp from the Williams Group to create a contemporary take on Anglo-Caribbean style. They then asked me to imagine clean, spare, tailored interiors with a pale neutral palette, modern lines, and natural materials. This would keep the emphasis on the impressive water views outside almost every room.

They also told me they wanted their home to be warm and welcoming, a breeze to entertain in, and to have the ability to easily accommodate their two grown sons on visits. It needed as well to be tough enough to withstand the owners' pair of playful golden retrievers—big dogs who are a big part of their lives.

With this brief in mind, I set my sights on a design scheme that would be as elegant as it was livable. I envisioned it defined by cerused-oak wood finishes, clean-lined furniture, sculptural pendant lights, antiqued brass hardware, and

OPPOSITE: The clean-lined, modern-classic interiors of this Naples, Florida, home take cues from the exterior's contemporary spin on Anglo-Caribbean architecture. PREVIOUS PAGES: I selected outdoor furniture that looks light and lovely—in keeping with the indoor scheme—even though each piece has enough heft to withstand extreme weather.

ABOVE: The entryway's stone consoles and black-framed mirrors provide contrast and structure.
OPPOSITE: The light and lovely atmosphere of the house begins with the foyer's statement-making floating staircase. Its wrought-iron balustrade previews the dark linear accents to come.

ABOVE, OPPOSITE, AND PREVIOUS PAGES: To keep the soaring living room feeling warm and inviting, I softened the tall windows with sheer linen curtains and selected a monumental black metal chandelier. The artwork over the fireplace is by Todd Murphy.

Simple touches of black punctuate the light spaces, preventing them from looking like they might up and float away.

black accents. The pale polished-stone floors and other light-colored surfaces, meanwhile, would stay free of scratches from the dogs. As in many mostly neutral interiors, texture would stand in for color here, and, because the homeowners didn't want much in the way of pattern, it would have to stand in for most printed textiles as well.

The architect set us all up for success, designing a house with a generous footprint, grandly proportioned rooms, and huge windows that take maximum advantage of the water views and let in tons of sunlight. The home's open, flowing spaces encouraged relaxed socializing and easy entertaining, too.

I made some of my earliest decorating decisions to infuse warmth and a human sense of scale into every one of the high-ceilinged spaces and to add a balance of softness and strength to the modern architectural lines. I hung flowing, ivory-hued linen curtains to frame views, offer privacy, and diffuse sunlight, and I suspended statement-making ceiling lights that helped fill the upper reaches of the seemingly sky-high rooms.

The personal style of the homeowner—who wears lots of tailored solids and has simple, classic taste—informed every inch of this house, but perhaps no space more than the living room.

Just look at the chandelier in the main living area. The open, circular, two-tiered candelabra-style piece combines classic, modern, and farmhouse influences—and it looked huge in the showroom. But it feels just the right size here, set below the oak-clad vaulted ceiling above tightly tailored, bone-colored upholstered seating.

To keep the bone-on-ivory-on-ecru-on-beige color scheme—or maybe I should call it a lack-of-color scheme—from feeling too cloudlike, I grounded nearly every room with a chunkily woven sisal rug in a caramel or driftwood hue.

I then introduced black or otherwise very dark brown accessories and art, most of them linear in nature. You'll find black curtain rods, blacked-steel light fixtures, and usually at least one piece of darkly stained wood-framed furniture in every room. All these dark accents function the same way a pop of a brighter pink or blue would in a more colorful scheme.

A mix of burnished pewter and brass, plus a wall of marble, set the kitchen sparkling—but in a muted way that's just right for this home's subtle scheme.

ABOVE AND OPPOSITE: I convinced the owners to paint all the windowpanes black, which you'd think would interrupt views, but because the dark-colored muntins and mullions all but disappear, it actually enhances them.

ABOVE AND OPPOSITE: With minimal touches of the palest blue, the family room departs ever so slightly from the color-free palette. Every house, even the most neutral one, needs some color somewhere. Here, I brought in the hues of water and sky. FOLLOWING PAGES: Mirrors flank the primary suite's bamboo-style four-poster bed, filling the room with light and reflections.

Designing with
TEXTURED NEUTRALS

MAKE IT PRETTY

Weave a captivating story. Grass cloth, seagrass, linen, chenille, bouclé, tweeds, herringbones—woven textiles are some of your best friends when it comes to adding visual interest to a neutral color scheme. They combine beautifully with sisal and jute rugs, plus furniture featuring rattan and caning.

Smoothness provides texture, too. Just as white can provide contrast and a visual break in an otherwise richly colored interior, sleek surfaces (polished stone, glass, and metal) do the same in a space filled with complex textures. Try using one to set off the other.

Layer it on. Beachy shades of sand, ivory, and ecru, along with the various textures mentioned above, can look great on their own, but they're even better in combination. Layer them the same way you would mix prints and patterns of different scales.

MAKE IT PRACTICAL

Organic-looking doesn't have to be natural. We all love natural materials, especially in a neutral interior. But they're not necessarily the easiest to maintain. I like to use washable, stainproof synthetic versions of materials like wicker and jute to make cleanup a breeze.

Try prints in place of texture. A print inspired by a patterned weave—like the herringbone one used for the pillows on the sofa in this sitting room—provides the appearance of texture without any of the nooks and crannies. That makes them simpler to wipe clean or even throw in the washer, in some cases.

Keep it light—but not too light. You know I like using pale neutrals to keep things looking pristine in places where sand, dust, and pollen can't be avoided. But don't go too light—all white or just off white. If you do, you'll find that every speck of dirt shows.

OPPOSITE: A sitting room in the guest wing provides extra space for quiet contemplation. FOLLOWING PAGES: The rich mix of textures in this bedroom makes its neutral palette anything but boring.

ABOVE AND OPPOSITE: In a home office, who wouldn't love this Rat Pack-style
speakeasy bar hidden behind a pair of doors? PREVIOUS PAGES: I like to invite a couple
to have one-on-one time by facing two chairs over an ottoman in a bedroom.

The vantage from the second floor
amplifies the water views.
You can literally see for miles and miles
from this bathroom, and the
relaxation that provides is unbelievable.

In an interior this spare, this neutral, the choice of every seemingly simple material, every shade of pale beige, every clean-lined silhouette, every touchable texture, becomes incredibly important. Each decision can feel pretty high stakes. There's very little margin of error. The trick is to be careful and considered in your approach and process and to think about the entire scheme at the same time as much as possible.

Thanks to doing just that—and to plenty of collaboration, too—we managed to make it all work with great success. In fact, the homeowners (as well as their sons and their dogs) were so pleased that after living in the house for a few months during their first winter in residence, they asked me to add a similar sense of space and light to their summer home in Colorado. I couldn't say yes fast enough.

Thanks to the almost floor-to-ceiling walls of glass surrounding it, the primary suite's tub makes anyone having a soak feel like they're afloat in the waters of Naples Bay.

Designing an
OUTDOOR KITCHEN

Bring the indoors out. To make this alfresco cooking and dining space feel of a piece with the design of the rest of the house, I carried the neutral hues, interesting textures, and linear black accents of the interior through to the outside.

Minimize the utilitarian. Since the dining area is open to an outdoor kitchen, I wanted to emphasize the beautiful, monumental table and substantial chairs by letting the culinary zone fade into the background. Using just a few similarly colored materials makes that happen.

Go green. The lushly verdant surroundings of this covered porch inspired me to style and accessorize the space with plenty of greenery. Fresh palm fronds arranged as centerpieces recall the trees that dot the property, as well as the woven textures throughout the interior.

Heavy does it. This house sits on an inlet off the Gulf of Mexico and not the open ocean, but it still needed to be hurricane-proof. Concrete tables and iron chairs are weighty enough to stay put in all but the strongest of gale-force winds.

Materials matter. This space had to be built for the outdoors even though I wanted to keep the look connected to the interior. The built-in teak cabinetry and shell stone–clad wall and grill hood can withstand the elements without showing signs of wear and tear.

Light up the night. Everyone loves candlelight and lantern light outside. Glass hurricane lamps ensure things stay lit in the wind. Hidden lights under the range hood provide task lighting without interrupting the sleek, natural look.

For a family of master chefs, the outdoor kitchen was as integral to the house as the inside one.

When you look out from the living room's wall of windows, the pool's far edge all but disappears into the bay, visually extending it.

Landscaping by Koby Kirwin, who also designed the pool, complements the tailored interiors and classically inspired architecture. In hot climates, light-colored stone or tile are a must for the patios and walkways surrounding a pool. Pale hues keep cooler in bright sun—and bare feet are sensitive!

San Jose

t his house in the San Jose neighborhood of Jacksonville, Florida, has such a sweet story behind it. One of its owners grew up nearby—he went to school with my son Max, in fact—then left for New York for twenty years. He made his career there, met his darling Mississippi-born future wife, got married, and had three precious kids. And then, just like that, they decided to move the whole family back to Jacksonville, so the little ones could attend the same school he did and have the same sort of idyllic Florida childhood.

He and his wife bought a big Georgian house, designed by architect Richard Skinner, right on the Saint Johns River. It's not so different from the one his family had, with a majestic red-brick exterior, a long dock reaching out into the water, and tons of connection to the river, thanks to pair after pair of French doors on the back of the house. These all open to broad brick patios, lawns, and the gently moving river beyond. This close relationship to the water made up a huge part of the owner's happy memories of his youth, and it very much informed my design.

Though his wife was also from the South, the owner knew that bringing her down to relatively small-town Jacksonville after years and years in New York was going to be something of a culture shock. When we first spoke, he said he had only one design directive for me: "Make her happy." (Smart man, right?) And so we did.

From the start, she and I saw eye to eye on what the house required. Traditional and grand, it needed an update and redesign to better suit her young, fun, and fairly casual family who love to entertain. We had to take the edge off its fancy, formal atmosphere. I'd never seen so many Corinthian columns in an interior—and I started by removing them all. I then simplified much of the other millwork and the fireplace mantels. We

OPPOSITE AND PREVIOUS PAGES: Easy access to the Saint Johns River defines nearly every room of this Jacksonville, Florida, home, so I borrowed from the colors of the river, sky, and surrounding greenery for the interior palette.

In a house with wonderful architectural details—dentil moldings, parquet floors—sometimes less is more when it comes to decorating.

kept the large dentil crown moldings throughout as well as the coffered ceilings but modernized them by colorfully painting the molding and inserting panels of textured wallpaper inside the coffers. The result is a house that's now more twenty-first-century glam than traditionally grand.

We agreed right away to introduce a lot of color throughout—usually in fairly light and often monochromatic ways that would keep each room feeling fresh and casual. We also brought in plenty of texture and pattern, much of the latter in the form of whimsical wall coverings. And we added in the sort of midcentury furniture, accents, and, especially, lighting that she loved. All that adds up to a definite sense of waterfront fun.

Some of the very best places to see all this are in the dining and the living rooms, which achieve the neat trick of simultaneously being two of the most formal and the most fun spaces here.

For the living room, I used a sweet botanical print in light blue and green—for both the wallpaper and fabric. (I love wrapping a room in a single pattern.)

Then, I added modernist flair with pale-aqua curved sofas and mid-twentieth-century chairs I found at an antique market in Parma, Italy. A surprisingly durable, Swedish flatweave carpet grounds the space; its colors coordinate with those on the walls, even as its graphic pattern contrasts with the florals.

OPPOSITE: While updating the house, I preserved classical details—like the foyer's dramatic dentil molding—then added midcentury and vintage-inspired furniture. PREVIOUS PAGES: The formal dining room became a lounge space that can be used day or night.

ABOVE, OPPOSITE, AND PREVIOUS PAGES: Wallpaper has made a comeback in a big way, and so has allover pattern. The formal living room in this house feels the furthest thing from fussy, thanks to both of those elements, plus the addition of vintage and newly made modernist furniture.

ABOVE: High-gloss color feels just right for festive cocktails. OPPOSITE AND PREVIOUS
PAGES: This multipurpose entertaining space is relatively casual, so we took the formal
edge off the classical millwork by painting it green and layering in woven textures.

Could this space be sweeter?
No. Is there such a thing as too
much pink? No again!

The dining room proves itself very pretty in pink, almost from head to toe. The homeowner and I had so much fun buying pink china and table linens to go with the scheme. A dramatic wall covering makes it appear that flowers, dotted with exotic birds, are gracefully climbing up the walls, reaching up toward the oversized dentil crown molding and ceiling papered in a marbleized print. Pink velvet–upholstered dining chairs with sexy, stiletto-style, hammered-bronze legs surround a thick-topped wooden table with a brass base. Hanging above is a white-glass Murano chandelier, which is both bold and soft at the same time.

Using modern light fixtures like that one helps achieve a look that blends the classical and the contemporary. Most all the lighting in the house combines traditional materials—brass frames, white or clear glass—with unexpected, statement-making, twenty-first-century shapes.

The homeowner may have been returning to Jacksonville to recreate his own small-town childhood, but he brought more than a little bit of New York flair—and a wife with great, sophisticated taste—back with him.

This room used to be an office, but because it's spacious and right off the kitchen, it seemed a perfect spot to move the formal dining area. Since it mostly gets used at night, it doesn't matter much that there's no water view.

Designing a
FAMILY ROOM

MAKE IT PRETTY

Prints charming. A riverfront family room is just the place for a whimsical, welcoming, and above all else *fun* atmosphere. Here, that vibe comes from the boldly patterned and brightly colored chinoiserie grass cloth wallpaper and ikat curtains. Looking at them, you just know you're in for a good time.

Define your zones. This large space had a beautiful, reclaimed limestone floor, which we left bare in the family room's breakfast nook (page 239) to make meal cleanup easy. In this seating area, a graphic Swedish flatweave rug grounds the space and connects the furniture together visually, while its grid pattern echoes the floor.

Take it personally. There's no better way to add warmth and a wonderfully lived-in look to a family room than with personal mementos. This room's wicker étagères (not pictured) hold favorite books and an array of framed family photos.

MAKE IT PRACTICAL

Make room for all. After falling out of favor for a while, the sectional sofa has made a comeback, especially in the homes of young families. This one feels cozy with three or thirteen people on it—and the homeowner has sent me photos of it with even more kids piled on, plus dogs.

The more indestructible, the better. Kids dance on this coffee table every night and jump from it to the sectional, too. Every upholstery fabric you see is a high-performance indoor-outdoor textile, and we chose dark colors to hide any stains that soak through. That Swedish flatweave rug is super durable, too, which is especially key, since the pool is right outside.

A place to stuff your stuff. A family room needs space for games and toys and stuffed animals and art supplies and who knows what all else the kids drag in. This one shows that storage can be stylish. Black sideboards (one of them seen on page 238) provide room to stow everything away.

When the homeowner fell in love with this bold chinoiserie wallpaper for the family room, and *then* went along with my idea to amp up the scheme even further with a pink ikat curtain fabric and a graphically patterned Swedish flatweave rug, I was thrilled.

ABOVE AND OPPOSITE: The family room also hosts a breakfast nook and everyday dining area with French doors that open to the pool. Between kids getting food everywhere and wet feet and bathing suits going every which way, everything here had to be indestructible—and it is, even if it doesn't look it.

A primary bedroom should be an oasis of serenity—and this one most certainly is. The decorating here keeps the emphasis on calm, with lots of solids and minimal contrast.

In the primary bedroom, we decided to go with a soothing, softer palette, incorporating lots of white, pale blues and greens, and a subtle print. My husband, Jim, designed the four-poster bed, and I found the mirrors, both in a chalk-white finish, while shopping the Paris flea markets.

ABOVE AND OPPOSITE: Pink and green are a classic combination—and for good reason. They always look good together. Here, I used the two hues in two different ways in a girl's bedroom and in the nursery.

Designing a
KID'S BEDROOM

MAKE IT PRETTY

Whimsical wall coverings work. This is one of my favorite wallpapers. It's so immersive; it makes any kid feel like they're scuba diving—especially if you paint the trim and pick window treatments to match the deep aqua color, as we did here.

Color sets the scene. Kids' rooms can handle bold juxtapositions of complementary colors. We used coral-colored accents throughout this room to contrast with the blue—and to create a tropical, reef-like feeling. The hues of the rug complete the scene.

Accessories continue the theme. Here, the rattan circular mirror—which also feels coastal—creates the suggestion of a ship's porthole over the headboard. The bed itself, finished with woven panels, has beachy appeal, while the leather-wrapped nightstand looks like a vintage trunk you might have brought on a cruise back in the day.

MAKE IT PRACTICAL

Give them room to roam. When it comes to furniture in a child's bedroom, it's important to decorate relatively sparsely. You want to leave plenty of space for fun, creative play. To that end, you'll also want to choose a soft (and easily cleaned) rug with a thick pad underneath.

Ask the kids for help. I like to find out a child's favorite color or colors before designing a room and to involve them a bit here or there—for example, letting them pick between one of two patterns I know will work. That gives them just enough agency to help them feel like they're making the space their own.

Expect them to grow. Take it from me, as both an interior designer and a mom (and a grandma). No matter how hard you try to decorate a room that will take your little kids up to college, it's only going to last till they're thirteen, and then they'll want everything to change. To ensure it'll last even that long, give them the freedom to pick the bedding they want, especially the sheets, and to change them every year or two.

The little boy I designed this room for loved blue, loved fish, and loved that his new house was going to be right on the water. I leaned into all of that with this scheme.

ABOVE: Yes, that's a slide down from the top bunk—the kids absolutely love it. OPPOSITE: If you're unsure about a color (as this homeowner was about yellow), try it as an accent in a guest room. FOLLOWING PAGES: Mix stripes and solids to make each stand out.

Jacksonville Beach

b y the time Jim and I got around to creating our waterfront dream house in Jacksonville Beach, we'd been married for thirty-eight years, had four grown kids, plus seven grandchildren—nearly all of them living nearby—and we'd already designed and built several homes for ourselves. We were finally ready to settle down and saw this as our ultimate forever house.

I grew up at the beach, but Jim was raised in Jacksonville proper, some thirty miles inland from the water, not so far from where we raised our own family. Waterfront living wasn't entirely foreign to us, since we'd had a house on Jacksonville's Saint Johns River, but once the kids were entirely out of the house, I said, "I'm really ready to get back to the beach." And, boy, was I.

We decided to move fast and bought a piece of land, then put up a little three-bedroom house in something like four months. The idea was to test the waters and get our feet wet, as it were, to help us figure out exactly what neighborhood, even what exact street, we wanted for our dream house. We discovered it in a private-feeling stretch of road that had plenty of peace and quiet, plus beach access and knockout water views over low dunes.

OPPOSITE: Using scalloped shingles, decorative paneling, window boxes, trellises, and a pergola, architect Mark Finlay, Jim, and I made the most of our Jacksonville Beach house's garage-focused facade. PREVIOUS PAGES: The east-facing third-floor deck is our preferred spot for alfresco happy hour.

Our foyer ensures that anyone arriving at our home makes a grand entrance. I love how the room lets you see all the way from one end of the house to the other.

Jim and I found a long, narrow piece of property here, then set about designing. Despite being married for as long as we have been, and despite working together for almost as long, we still don't always have the exact same aesthetic sensibility or point of view on a shared project. But we did agree right away that we wanted something other than a typical Florida-style house. Instead, we gravitated more toward a Northeastern look. So, we turned to Connecticut-based architect Mark Finlay, whose work we had admired for a long time.

Together, we came up with a four-bedroom, three-story, traditionally styled shingle-clad beach house that incorporated just enough classical elements—columns framing the entry porch, a pediment over a top-story window, Chippendale railings—to make it feel like a descendent of the turn-of-the-twentieth-century beach "cottages" of places like Newport, Rhode Island, and New York's Hamptons.

Inside, Jim worked his magic. He turned the interiors out with coffered and tracery-adorned ceilings, walls paneled in carved wood and plaster, and wide, dramatic moldings, some featuring seashell details. For the very center of the

The interior architecture Jim created for the first floor of our three-story oval stair hall impresses with neoclassical details. The subdued, low-contrast color palette we finished it with keeps the whole thing feeling timeless.

To balance the gravitas of this stair landing's more traditional furniture, I selected casual accessories, including a pair of French plaster lamps, sculptural seashells, and pieces of coral.

257

Jim absolutely outdid himself with our house's three-story central stair hall. He poured his heart and soul into its design—and it shows.

house, he designed a show-stopping, three-story oval staircase topped by a cupola with windows that flood the steps with beautiful light. His staircases never disappoint, and this one is just extraordinary.

But here's the thing—and I'm not complaining, I swear I'm not—I made only one request when we started this dream house. I just wanted a simple white cottage. And what I ended up with was something I jokingly refer to as Versailles by the Sea (aka VBTS). I saw it happening along the way, and I know I could have stopped it, but I guess I just put my head in the sand. The house ended up way fancier than I wanted it to be. Jim, bless him, just couldn't help himself.

That all meant that when it came to decorating, my job became to kind of take the edge off the formality. Jim had built into the interior architecture nearly all the focal points and grand gestures the house could handle. My work didn't need to be dramatic or make a statement. It just needed to make our home feel softer and prettier. Basically, I had to do what I do best, if I do say so myself.

No matter the angle you view it from, the sinuous set of steps Jim created offers a visual feast. Its wavelike undulations form a cozy alcove on the ground level, and on the floors above, it makes you feel like you're heading to the heavens.

ABOVE, OPPOSITE, AND PREVIOUS PAGES: In the living room, we mixed a variety of seaside motifs, from the pale blue and ivory palette to the shell-shaped sconces to the rope, wicker, and bamboo furniture. Decorative painter Michael Gilbert created the floor's faux-marble mosaic Vitruvian scroll detail.

I started with the color palette, landing on light, water-inspired hues that mixed blues, greens, and grays, then used plenty of warm neutrals like ivory and sand. The material mix of natural fibers brings depth and even more warmth, as do the overstuffed upholstered seating and playful prints and patterns, especially the feminine-feeling florals and botanicals that I found for almost every room.

While we were planning the house, we bought some wonderful pieces of vintage and antique furniture and accessories on trips to England, France, Italy, and locally, too. These pieces—including the living room's English rococo–style shell-framed mirror and midcentury-modern Perspex desk and the stair landing's stone console, which has a top supported by a trio of carved dolphins—all help connect the decorating back to the details of the classical architecture.

In the end, it all worked out, and, ultimately, if I'm being honest, I suppose the house is less the *Palace* of Versailles by the Sea and more like the Cottage of Versailles.

And it didn't all just work out for me. Jim loves it too, of course, and our kids and grandchildren, as well. Don't let the neat and tidy, cool and calm pictures here fool you. This whole place is a playground. I hadn't realized the house had a circular loop of hallways until our grandchildren turned the place into a racetrack. And the library? It basically becomes their rec room, with the cabinets under the bookshelves holding toys. The pool, patios, and porches, meanwhile, are the equivalent of the kids' club at a waterfront beach resort. And me? Well, I wouldn't have it any other way.

The textural white-on-white artwork by French artist Jane Puylagarde, which we commissioned in Paris, inspired much about the room's scheme, not least the wall panels embedded with plaster seashells that Jim designed.

OPPOSITE: Our wood-paneled library turns into a playroom for the grandkids. Cabinets below the bookshelves—finished by decorative painter Bob Christian—conceal tons of toys.
ABOVE: Yes, it's Florida, and yes, it gets just cold enough here to make a fireplace a necessary luxury.

Designing a
MULTIPURPOSE LIBRARY

MAKE IT PRETTY

Books come first—and last. Bookcases are best for books. If you don't have any and don't plan to get any, then shelves can end up just looking cluttered with stuff. When you do have books, though, and it comes time to arrange your shelves, you always want to start by placing your larger decorative accessories (ceramic vessels, frames, and other objects), and then fill in with books.

Bring the brightness. We lit up our library here every which way—with picture lamps over artwork, a chandelier, sconces, and LED strip lights on the back of the shelves. All of that, plus the fireplace—which we love, even in Florida, on relatively cool nights—provides the place with a warm, gentle glow.

Literary allusions. Let a room's purpose guide its design. The cypress wood paneling, cabine-try, and shelving that Jim designed immediately give this space the atmosphere of a classic home library, and the wall covering we found for the ceiling echoes the look of marble-ized papers used in traditional bookbinding.

MAKE IT PRACTICAL

Storage matters. Ensure shelves are deep enough and tall enough for your books—at least twelve inches deep and high, but you'll want to measure your books—unless you're building shelves to be adjustable. Cabinets below keep things looking neat and provide space for photo albums, pillows and blankets, and, in our case, the grandkids' toys.

Game on. To help a library get used by avid readers and nonreaders alike, I always like to add a games table if you have the space for it. They're so en vogue right now—and for good reason. Whether you use one for chess, checkers, Monopoly and other board games, or puzzles, a games table really stretches a library's use.

Comfort is king. You can have all the best books in the world, lovely lighting, and a perfect sense of calm, but if the furniture in your library isn't cozy enough to linger in, no one is going to use the room. Here, we went with overstuffed down-filled pieces that people want to sit in forever.

We skipped a formal dining room because we realized we only ever used our old one on Christmas Eve. Instead, just before the holiday every year, we turn the library into a festive setting with three big, round tables, where our whole family dines together.

With its brass fittings, marble counters,
dramatic bronze range hood, walls tiled from
floor to ceiling, and modern barstools,
our kitchen feels like it has no timestamp,
which is something I always strive for.

270

ABOVE: The contemporary wicker and bamboo chairs set at the kitchen's vintage French-oak table are super lightweight, which lets us move them around easily. OPPOSITE: We activated what could have been a passthrough space—the wide, frequently used hallway connecting the library and kitchen—by adding a fun and fancy bar on one wall. Now, the space gets plenty of use, and it acts as a pool bar, too, thanks to the French doors that open to the backyard.

MAKE IT PRETTY

All that glitters. Adding a bar to a room—in our case, we have one in the hall between the library and the kitchen—always makes a space feel special and festive, even when there isn't a party going on. All the glassware, bottles, and polished metal items bring the shimmer. I like to up the ante with mirrors, high-gloss paint or lacquer, and sparkling counters.

Big spend, small space. Things that are expensive usually look it, and they're prettier for it. Because of a bar's petite size, you can use big-ticket materials—for counters, back-splash, cabinetry, and shelves—without break-ing the bank. You'll need every element in such a minimal quantity, things just don't add up to all that much.

Art for art's sake. A painting, photograph, or work on paper goes a long way toward adding sophistication. By centering a piece in the space, you can provide a wonderful focal point and a conversation starter for guests while you make drinks.

MAKE IT PRACTICAL

Appliance logic. I always like to have a bar sink—not for actually doing dishes or even getting a glass of water—but because it's a convenient place to pour a drink out. It also gives the whole setup an air of authenticity. Beyond that, you'll want a mini-fridge and an ice maker, plus a dish-washer if you can fit one.

Ice flows. About that ice maker: Make sure you get one that creates cubes the size and shape you like. There are so many different kinds to pick from these days. And be sure to find out how much noise it makes—many can be quite loud when they dump out the ice.

Lower maintenance. When it comes to countertops, as pretty as marble can be, it's also quite porous and not the greatest when you have acidic lemon and lime juice spritzing around, to say nothing of red wine spills. You could also consider unlac-quered metals that wear patina well, rather than those that need polishing.

Using open shelving in the mirror-backed bar ensures that glassware is always easy to grab and that it's always on display to add sparkle to this dynamic space.

Colefax and Fowler released a new blue, gray, and ivory colorway of its famous Bowood pattern—one of my favorite prints of all time—just in time for me to use it all over the primary bedroom.

276

ABOVE: In the primary bathroom, the pattern of the tile floor echoes the lines of the Chippendale railing on the porch that's visible through the large window. OPPOSITE: A bifold screen of framed botanical artwork hides a TV while also offering easy access to it.

The bedroom we designed
for our London-based
daughter and son-in-law
has a tropical feeling,
thanks to a Gracie wall
covering customized with
imagery of alligators,
live oak trees, and palms.
These reference the
flora and fauna of our
little corner of the world.

This is the room where
our grandchildren get to
stay when they sleep over.
All seven of them have
been known to use the bed
hangings—which match
the fabric-tented vaulted
ceiling—to swing from
mattress to mattress.

ABOVE AND OPPOSITE: The house has plenty of indoor space, but we basically live outside when there's good weather. Any time of day, you can find us at one of these two tables, watching the kids in the pool or marveling at the dunes and ocean.

Acknowledgments

As I reflect on this book, my fifth, the first thing that comes to mind is that putting each of these volumes together has been a wonderful way to chronicle my career and document my work along the way. It's also been a great way for me to show my appreciation for everyone who makes this work possible.

First and foremost among those to thank are my employees. These projects simply could not happen without the tremendously talented group of people behind me every step of the way. We laugh, we cry, and we work really hard—but we still always manage to have a lot of fun, too. We have a joke at our company holiday party, where I say "please" and "thank you," and that's supposed to count as appreciation for the whole year. But here I'd like to say a sincere thank-you to everyone who helps me every day: project managers, store employees, computer renderers, bookkeepers, and warehouse and delivery staff. Everybody's contribution is very important. Every curtain we hang in an interior, every piece of furniture that we sell in one of our stores, it all gets touched by many, many hands before it ends up in someone's house. That's something a lot of people don't realize.

I also want to express my appreciation to Abrams for believing in me and for continuing to support and showcase my decorating work. Special thanks to editorial director Shawna Mullen for always being so bright and cheerful, and to the rest of the team, including design manager Danny Maloney, managing editor Krista Keplinger, and production manager Larry Pekarek.

Much gratitude as ever to book designers Doug Turshen and Steve Turner. They always do an amazing job, as do the photographers and stylists who can take any room and make it look magical. Thank you as well to writer and editor Andrew Sessa for making the process of writing this book and my two previous ones easy and seamless. With him, something that could be a struggle for me is always a total pleasure.

I'm lucky to work with many brilliant architects who also make collaborating a pleasure. I've learned a tremendous amount from each of you. The same is true of the incredible contractors and builders I work with, people who keep everything about these projects organized and moving forward. In these houses, every element matters, and so I'm grateful to all the talented artisans and craftspeople—decorative painters, upholsterers, millworkers, curtain makers, and wallpaper hangers, to name just a few. Your eye for detail is not lost on me.

Thank you to all of my clients for your trust and confidence, especially my repeat clients. Our relationships are what drive me to keep going and get better and more creative every day.

And, finally, thank you to my family: my husband, Jim; our children; and our grandchildren—Jack, Henry, Rosie, Violet, Brody, Joe, and Liam. You all are my greatest inspiration and the joy of my life.

Editor: Shawna Mullen
Designer: Doug Turshen with Steve Turner
Design Manager: Danny Maloney
Managing Editor: Krista Keplinger
Production Manager: Larry Pekarek

Library of Congress Control Number: 2024942511

ISBN: 978-1-4197-6803-3
eISBN: 979-8-88707-023-0

Printed and bound in China
10 9 8 7 6 5 4 3 2 1

Abrams books are available at special discounts when purchased in quantity
for premiums and promotions as well as fundraising or educational use.
Special editions can also be created to specification.
For details, contact specialsales@abramsbooks.com or the address below.

Abrams® is a registered trademark of Harry N. Abrams, Inc.

ABRAMS The Art of Book
abramsbooks.com

195 Broadway
New York, NY 10007
abramsbooks.com